That Little Girl

a collection of poetry

Alice Smith

Produced by:

in memory of my mother

ALICE   PROBASCO LUPTON

April 26, 1927 - August 31, 2017

What people are saying about Alice Smith's Poetry

Alice Smith's poems are like the roof crashing in or the ground swelling up. In one line or a handful of words, Smith is able to transform the everyday into the sacred and the beautiful. That is the gift of poetry, and Smith reminds us to pay sweet attention to the small things before us. That's where the meaning is.

David Cook - columnist, Chattanooga Times Free Press

Alice Smith lures us across the threshold of her secret inner world, a world which we quickly recognize as our own. Her poetic offerings bring our own secrets to consciousness where they can be embraced and honored. Good poems serve this essential mysterious purpose, and these soul-full selections meet the test.

Jerry R. Wright - Jungian Analyst

These poems are about this very moment, and yet they also (and sometimes at the same time) go way back, way forward, and way deep--with beautiful, fresh metaphor and surprise at all the right places. Once you start you are pulled through to the end. What a pleasure to read and learn about yourself— taught by the poems, the art, of a poet who is exploring everything within reach, and learning about herself.

Clyde Edgerton, author of *Walking Across Egypt* and *The Night Train*

Alice Smith's collection of spare, beautiful poems is a faithful record of a conscious life. We view the ever-changing circle of her world, as love brings joy, then pain, then joy again. From child to girl to wife and mother, a woman's entire journey is mapped in these pages, and an enviable wisdom is born. As all good poetry does, Smith's poetry has made me look at my own life in a more attentive and appreciative way.

Lee Smith, author
Hillsborough, NC

Alice Smith's voice is one to be heard. Her words evoke feelings of wisdom and truth, of delight and regret as she writes about coming full circle in life. After cancer surgery she describes herself as "somewhat diminished and somehow enlarged." Her words bring the reader to despair, then describe hope and the beautiful shining moments of life so clearly it is palpable.

Ferris Kelly Robinson, author of *Making Arrangements* and *Dogs and Love - Stories of Fidelity*

TABLE OF CONTENTS

Introduction

It has been some time since I last put out a book of poetry. These past few years have been very emotional, both personally and politically. Personally I have lived through my sister's bladder cancer, her husband's pancreatic cancer and death, my mother's breast cancer and death, and my own breast cancer, chemo, surgery and radiation. As for political emotions, anyone living in this country can't help but be aware of the tension and division that exist. Writing has been a wonderful way for me to deal with all the emotional upheaval. Whenever I sit down to write I am struck by the unexpected joy and gratitude that is intermingled with the pain and suffering. I certainly wouldn't have chosen many of the things that have happened over the last several years, but it is the unchosen that has taught and given me so much.

I have resisted putting out another book because I am unable to figure out how to deal with the copyright issues of pairing my

poems with artwork the way I can do on my online poetry page. There I have access to a vast array of art I can post along side my poems, and to me the combination of words and images is far more powerful than words alone. In this book, however, you will have to settle for words only, but if you would like to see how art enhances the poetry please visit my poetry page.
www.facebook.com/AliceLuptonSmithPoetry

    I have had many people tell me that they don't even like poetry but can relate to what I write. I am very grateful for all my readers be they poetry haters or poetry lovers. Thank you, readers, for your continuing interest and support. Thank you!

Alice Smith

THAT LITTLE GIRL

I found her cracked and crumpled
hidden in a dresser drawer.
She is four maybe five.
I know the eyes, a grayish blue
though the picture is simply sepia.
I see the wispy frizz atop her head,
a bus token pinned to her collared dress,
lips slightly parted,
and a smile almost there.
Is she contented or afraid?
I can't remember now.
I'll put her back inside my drawer
and take her out from time to time
so I can see that little girl
who has a home inside of mine.

FALL

Afraid she might be noticed,
   she hid her frizzy fear
   in the corner cardboard kitchen
   playing all alone
   that kindergarten year.
The pageant produced a panic
   when she was chosen out of all
   to parade behind the king and queen
   and play the part of fall.
Winter, spring and summer
   wore sparkly sequined tutus.
Winter twinkled in snowy white.
Spring and summer glittered
   in different shades of green,
   but nothing shined on fall.
Some seamstress mother
   created the humiliation
   the other season wore.
Homemade layers
   of multi colored netting
   lay limp and lifeless.
Like autumn leaves
   she wanted to be raked away.
Her fear was confirmed,
  "The Ugliest of All"
   as she trailed behind the king and queen
   the night they made her fall.

THE DREAM OF ME

I was dreamed
long before
I was born.
All of me
is in the dream,
but some of me
is hard to see.
I often cling
to what I want to see
and miss a piece
of what is there for me.
The dream is filled
with miracles and magic,
suffering and sorrow,
the best of me,
the worst of me,
the absolutely all of me.
Now I lay me down to sleep.
I pray my dreams
will help me keep
unfolding.

THE WHOLE STORY

I do not know the whole story.
I remember nothing
from the prologue
or the preface
or even from the first few pages.
All I know is I am here
over half way through for sure,
but how much more there is to go
is not for me to know.
What chapter am I living?
Will the story slowly drag along
until the final page is nothing
but an anticlimax,
or will the ending take me by surprise?
Will there be an epilogue
and then an afterward?
The more I ask
the more I know
I do not know the whole story.

In Praise of Common Things

There's extraordinary beauty
in an ordinary day
when you let the little things
take your breath away.

an apple on the counter...
the coffee in your mug...
the children's make believe...
an unexpected hug...
sunshine in the winter...
a cozy little nest...
fireside conversation...
your monkey mind at rest...
singing in the shower...
smelling chocolate pie...
tromping through the leaves...
gazing at the sky...

When you view the world
in a fascinating way
there's extraordinary beauty
in an ordinary day.

THE GIFTED NATURE OF LIFE

I give thanks
for Mother Nature
assuring me at dusk
she'll paint the morning sky
with yet another day.

I give thanks
for my imagination
to see a scene I have not lived
and take me off to territories
barely known to me.

I give thanks
for quiet places
where I can hear the inner notes
play mellow music
lost in the percussion of daily life.

I give thanks
for unexpected anger
that cracks the tranquil surface
to free me from the falsity
that I am in control.

I give thanks
for uncontrollable laughter,
that irresistibly contagious burst
which has the power to cure
a multitude of ills.

I give thanks
for uninvited sadness
showing me how to find the beauty
in the hidden stuff
that makes me weep.

I give thanks
for the ups and downs
and ins and outs of life
for without the down and out
the up and in would lose their meaning.

I give thanks!

THE HALLOWED HUSH

The sacred place of emptiness
is full of powerful presence.

Let us take the time
to undo all the doing.

Let us clear away the clutter
letting go of all distraction.

Let us sit in silence
long enough to hear the whispers from within.

Let us move into the realm of being
and sit in the sphere of aloneness.

Let us heed the hallowed hush
hidden under life's percussion.

This sacred place of emptiness
is full of powerful presence.

IMAGINATION

Pounce into your own imagination.
It's a mystical, marvelous place!
There are no rules.
There are no boundaries.
There are no limits at all.
You are your own inventor
recreating,
rearranging,
re-imagining what is there,
finding something everywhere.
Make it up.
Make it vast.
Make it more than more.
Or break it down,
and build it back
better than before.
No one here can stop you
from bouncing through the wonder
and playing with the power
of your imagination.

THE GRAYNESS OF SAMENESS

The seduction of sameness
pulls us in
and holds us
in the grayness,
staving off
the vibrancy of change,
white-washing
the dark hues of the depths
and the shimmering shades of the numinous.
Sameness is painted
with a stroke of safety,
never veering outside the lines
with a splash of spontaneity
or a brilliant stroke of creativity.
Perhaps today's the day
to break away from gray,
pull out the magic markers
and draw on something new.

BEYOND YOUR PANE

If you never leave,
this place will become
a dilapidated safe-house
surrounding you with impregnable familiarity.
But if you clutch the cape of courage
and venture down the path
that leads beyond what you can see
through your wavy windowpane,
you're bound to stumble into newness
and may be battered a bit
when you reach the mountain top,
but you will have a wider way
to view what lies ahead;
and if you end up back where you began
it's not the same as never leaving.

BLESS THE GROUND

Before sailing across oceans
and conquering mountains
take time to notice
the ground on which you stand.
Kick off your shoes
removing the barrier
between your sole
and what is underneath.
Squish your toes in the grass
and thank the soil from which it sprouts.
Be grateful for the green,
then bow and bless the ground.

TRIP TO NOWHERE

I took a trip to nowhere
and found it filled
with everything.
A very wise conductor
led me through
the unattended fields
of shadow and shame
before I was brought
to the quiet station of stillness.
This depot in the deep
was dark then light
then filled with fright
that mellowed into muted calm.
I wanted to stay
for more than awhile,
but the time to leave had arrived.
Before I pulled away
I packed a piece of peace
to take as a reminder
of my memorable trip to nowhere.

TRAVEL LIGHT

What will I carry,
and what will I leave behind?

I'd like to travel light,
and my personal baggage
is heavy enough
so there isn't any need
to carry the weight of the world.

These old, worn out resentments
stashed away inside
are so unnecessary.
If I unpack their meaning
perhaps they'll find a way
of landing in Goodwill.

When I travel into foreign places
I'll take the kindness dictionary
that someone offered me.
It's understood in every land
no matter what the language.

I'll give away my hang ups
and keep the key to wonder
so I can enter territories
padlocked in my dreams.

I'll pack up pleasant memories,
at least the ones that still remain.
It seems I've lately lost a lot,
but then again
I said I'd like to travel light.

WHERE OH WHERE

Where oh where have my little ones gone?
I almost miss the mayhem.
Where are the toys?
Where is the noise?
Where are the dirty clothes?
I miss the squeal.
I miss the feel.
I miss the make-believe.
I'll wrap delights they left with me
and keep them close at hand.
If peace and quiet get to me
I'll open up my box of joys
and let the memories bounce about
bringing back the noise.

CHANGE

Change is in the air,
sometimes subtle
but always there
like the oxygen we breathe
unconsciously
without notice
without thought.

Uproarious transformation
clearly catches our attention
blowing us about
whipping us inside out
like a tornado
whirling through the air
coming from who knows where.

Be it calm or be it chaotic,
there's no way to avoid
inevitable alteration
for with every breath we take
and every move we make,
change is in the air.

A Colorful Country

The land in which we live
is a colorful bazaar
of closely held beliefs.
Let us hold our differences
with patience and respect.
Let us all be faithful
to better angels of our nature.
Let us value our diversity
and talk of possibility
converting animosity into animation.

BIG AND SMALL

Our lives are filled
with powerful and petite,
monumental and minuscule,
conspicuous and concealed.
We tend to notice mammoth
but overlook the little things.
We hear the loud and lusty
while missing out on undertones.
We understand the obvious
but fail to notice nuance.
Let our eyes see what is in front of us
then look for the ignored.
Let our ears hear the sound and solid
then listen for the innuendoes.
Let our minds grasp the plain and simple
then search for subtleties.
Let our hearts harbor big and small
and find a way to hold it all.

BIT BY BIT

I cannot transform
the whole wide world.
I can only grapple
with bits and pieces
of me,
but if a morsel
of me
is modified
the whole
is also altered.

Land Like a Loom

How I wish we could create
a land that functions like a loom
where we continue stretching,
not ripping
things   apart.

Sinking into cynicism
or fleeing to idealism
removes the crucial tension
that holds the piece in place,
but using threads of give and take
intertwined with strands of hope
could help us to reweave
the highly valued fabric
of our common life together.

The Company of Strangers

In the song and dance of common life
we sing and sway
in the company of strangers.
Let the city sidewalk
be a dancing lesson.
No slamming into one another
or slinging folks aside,
just speeding up and slowing down,
veering left then veering right,
getting where we want to go
more or less in time.
In the common life of song
we play in different keys,
voice our sundry sounds
making quite a noise
with such a motley crew.
Let us learn to take a stand
but never demonize.
Let us learn to voice our truth
and try to harmonize.
Let us dance, and let us sing.
Let a common theme take wing
as we the people celebrate
the company of strangers.

FINDING FORGIVENESS

I find an open crack
in my over written tragedy
and step into a larger place.
This re-imagined space
leavened with forgiveness
creates a different story
from the version filled with feelings
that cut me to the quick.
Now that I am here
I wonder why I dawdled there.
Oh the wasted time I spent
tangled in vindictiveness
and blinded by pathetic pride
instead of building bridges
that lead to understanding,
acceptance and compassion.
When I find myself again
entangled and unbending
help me to unwind.
Clear my blurry eyes,
and give me sharper vision
to see connective overpasses
leading to forgiveness.

PERHAPS THE FENCE WILL FALL

If I descend
to my hands and knees
and dig through
my personal patch
of closely held opinions,
and you
who live on the other side
agree to do the same,
who knows what sort of soil
our digging will unearth.
If we loosen the land
perhaps the fence will fall,
and we might soon discover
a fertile circle
of common ground.

MIDDLE GROUND

We want to be
wowed by wonder
knocked to our knees,
tickled to tears,
and possessed by passion
all the time,
but we're not.
We don't want to be
devastated by disaster,
crushed by criticism,
trampled by tragedy,
or lost in loneliness
all the time,
and we're not.
All of us
have glimpsed the glorious
and felt the frightful,
seen the splendid
and tasted the terrible,
but most of the time
we muddle around
in the middle.

Rock and Roll for Peace

I marched,
and then I marched again
although I'd never marched before.
That part of me that yearns for peace
became a marching activist.

Peace is not passivity.
Peace requires
an active mind,
a searching soul,
a vivid voice,
a mighty move!

Let us come together
to really rock and roll.
Let us fling a fist of peace
with fingers pointing to beyond.
Let us raise our voices
and make a mighty move
with activated minds
and ever searching souls
dancing through the streets
for peace, let's rock and roll!

THERE'S HOPE IN THE QUESTIONS

We live in a wounded world
where blood is spilled
and lives are lost,
and it happens time and again.
How can we as a people
transform our angry nation?
Can the tears of grief be the tie that binds?
Can suspicions disappear?
Can compassion be the bridge to healing?
Can hurtful hatred cease?
Can we nurture all the neglected
lost in the land of the free?
Can we learn from a time of suffering
and become the home of the brave?

TIME FOR A BREAK

When absolutely stuck in place
it may be time to take a break.
The sticky question is but how?
break in?
break out?
break up?
break down?
break a rhythm?
break a rule?
break open?
break through?
break a hold?
break a heart?
break away?
break apart?
No matter what the break
some sort is necessary
to shift the broken pieces
into a mending place.

LEAD ME ON

Take me as I am.
Lead me on.
Lead me on
through the night of mystery
into the morning song.
Take me as I am
filled with hope,
filled with fear.
Take me as I am,
and lead me on.
If I stumble in the dark
sing the notes
loud and strong.
Sing 'em out.
Sing 'em clear.
Sing the notes
so I can hear.
Lead me on.
Lead me on
through the night of mystery
into the morning song.

LOCKED INSIDE

That locked interior
room of mine
is filled with luminous angels
and terrifying beasts.
They are always there,
but I'm hardly aware
of their explosive presence.

The bright shining halo
beckons and beams,
but I fail to believe
it belongs to me.
It bears my name
and is mine to claim
if only I'll open the door.

The demon creatures
claw and chew
but beg to be stroked and tamed.
I made them wild
by pushing them down
and locking them in
so I need to open the door.

Locked inside
is a volatile place
for treasure and trouble alike.
It is clear
I alone
have the key to that room.
Will I use it or let it rust?

A REFRAMED WORLD

How dare those muted memories
reappear in living color!
Whenever they come calling
she turns up the music
and dances with herself,
whirling through
the impressionistic scene
painted by her own brush.
Layers of whitewash
dull the demons into shadows
lurking underneath
where they can fade away
for a spell
leaving her alone
in her reframed world.

A SWIRL OF GRACE

Why do I cling
to the same old thing
and thwart its falling apart?
The chaos caused by coming undone
invites my soul
to listen at a deeper level
and notice notes
that signal modulation.
But instead of heeding transformation
I deny the invitation,
tighten my controls
and cling to outworn certitudes
that shield me from conversion.
What I need is courage.
What I need is guidance.
What I need is patience
to float in the darkest dark
until a swirl of grace swoops me up
and whirls me into something wholly new.

BROKEN HEARTS

If a heart is brittle
it will shatter when it's broken
and explode into a million pieces
inflicting untold pain.
A brittle broken heart
is stuck with hurt still unresolved.
The shards keep wounding the wounded
and continue wounding others.

But if a heart is supple
it can be broken open,
strong enough
to bear the suffering,
patient enough
to hold the tension,
limber enough
to bend toward compassion
and resilient enough
to become a source of healing.

MODULATE THE MOOD

The rhythm is frenetic
no break
not even a half note rest.
The angry drummer
of unattended stress
is pounding madly,
trying like crazy
to get your attention,
and the worn out weariness blues
have finally taken over.
Take a breath.
Take a break.
Take the time
to modulate the mood
into a different key.
Pay attention to the drummer.
Then let the sound of laughter
weave its way into your song
brightening the blues
and mellowing the mad.
Look for dotted half notes
slowing down the pace.
Ah, the beat is better now.
You're in a different place.

CLIMB INTO MYSTERY

Beware the cell of certainty
with concrete blocks walling you in
and windows rodded with rigidity
forever obstructing your views.
When you want more
than safety and security
doubt begins to sprout
pushing through the crevices,
crashing through the cracks
till the walls come tumbling down.
Take a step into the questions
that pave the path to parts unknown
and circle 'round to somewhere unexplored
and something unfamiliar.
Reach beyond what you can see
and touch a piece of the invisible
grabbing hold of you
and spinning you around
giving you a peek
of glorious and gruesome,
of underneath and inside out.

You won't get all the answers,
just tiny little glimpses
of what it's all about
when you finally make the choice
to wander through the wonder
and climb into the mystery.

GOD

A powerful, intimate mystery
before and beyond,
around and among,
wondrously woven within.
I am in love with the mystery,
in awe of the power,
in need of the intimacy.

How presumptuous of me
to try to describe
the absolutely indescribable
so let me bow
and simply allow
myself to be aware
of what is always there.

MYSTERY LANE

I don't want
all the answers
for what if the answers
are wrong?
Fill me up
with questions
that blaze the trail to somewhere
then find a way to wonderland.
Let me dabble in doubt
and wander about
feeling my way from here to there.
Keep me off
the cul-de-sac of certainty,
and point the way
to Mystery Lane
that never ever ends.

QUESTIONS

How will you live your life?
Will you walk in sturdy shoes
staring straight ahead
stepping on whatever lives beneath
making sure to reach what lies beyond?
Or will you gaze below
and see the tiny buttercups
scattered through the green
then get down on your knees
and pick a bunch of gold
to take as a reminder of life's little wonders?
Will you listen to the works
of master composers and blue grass bands
so many times that every note
is etched into your brain?
Or will you sing a song only known by you
that changes every time
you take another shower?
Will you keep in mind the famous words
of thinkers, poets and prophets
spilling them for all to hear
whenever they are needed?

Or will you forget what came before you
and scribble something thought to be your own
only to find it was better said by others
many years ago?
How will you live your life?
Will you try to stick with answers
or wander through the questions?

Right Outside Your Window

The desire for something new
lives somewhere
in the curtained corners
of your being,
but the seduction of safety
holds you captive
to the everyday grayness
of unsensational sameness.
If you feel a sense of emptiness
follow that twinge of fearlessness
that leads to a colorful place
filled with more than plenty.
Your courage will be rewarded
for once you have sensed
the richness of risk
you'll raise the shade
and be amazed
at kaleidoscopic wonder
right outside your window.

Seeds of Doubt

The growing season has begun
when seeds of doubt
begin to sprout
spreading tiny roots
beneath the surface
and forming something new.
Without a doubt
the hardened soil of certainty
becomes a barren place.
Nurture niggling questions
disturbing the status quo.
Plant them in the deep
and feel the ground below
shift and move a bit
as something new begins to grow.

SOUL HAIKU

Keys to enter soul:
prayerfully open the heart,
and unlock the mind.

LONELINESS AND SOLITUDE

The stale air
hanging in the lounge of loneliness
reeks of memories rotting
as they linger past their expiration date.
A steamy scent
of never lived desires
simmers under the surface
leaving a whiff of woe is me.
Oh to be delivered from this loneliness!

But the sweet breeze
wafting though the solarium of solitude
is spiced with fragrance of appreciation
for precious time alone.
The balm of yesterday's bouquet
and tomorrow's possibilities
are faintly floating in and out
enhancing the aroma of aloneness.
Oh to be surrounded by this solitude!

SACRAMENTAL TEARS

For everything that's taken
something new is given.
I see
how youthful passion
can gracefully shrink
into an ever expanding perspective.
I feel
how nimble knees
that used to run with ease
can take a bow to mental flexibilities.
I understand
how flowering energy
can wilt into the space
the withering has created
for fertile reflection.
Yes, for everything that's taken
something new is given
so let me shed
some sacramental tears
for the inescapable mingling
of loss and gain.

LOOKING FOR SOME LIGHT

I think I can.
I think I can.
Right now I think I can't.
Who am I to say
I can't?
The world is filled with billions
far worse off than I.
My immediate woes
are but a faint whisper
to those who wonder
when or if
their children will be fed
or their loved ones
will be dead
so should I raise my head,
sing a song,
dance along,
wear ribbons in my hair,
make believe that life is fair?
I can't pretend
to ignore my plight,
and maybe soon
I can see some light.
I hope I can.
I hope I can.

Halfway Intentions

I half way intended
to deliver delights
to the neighbor across the way,
half way imagined
wearing a red satin dress
to a boring business bash,
half way meant
to hand a hundred dollars
to that hungry, homeless man,
half way envisioned
running down the beach
completely in the nude,
half way thought about
courageously stepping
outside of my safe little world,
half way considered
speaking my mind to those
who might think me crazy,
but so far I haven't
lived up to my intentions.
If tomorrow I'm squashed or captured,
trampled or raptured
I'll never live out
the half of what I intended.

Such a Kind

I am sitting in the dark
viewing the projection.
Unexpected words
from a poignant
British comedy
seem to unravel me.
Find a person who is kind.
Such a quest
had never crossed my mind.
I blink the blurring
from my eyes
and swallow the lump
settling in my throat
for here I am
sitting next to such a kind.

THE GIFT

The gift that you have given me
is the greatest gift of all,
more precious than diamonds,
more treasured than gold,
richer than chocolate,
sweeter than cream.
The gift that you have given me
enlivens, enlightens,
enlarges, enriches.
There is no box included
for that would be confining.
The gift that you have given me
is to love me as I am.
No questions asked,
no improvements needed,
I'm loved just as I am!

PLAIN AND SIMPLE

I must drop the trappings
and tear away the wrappings
for only when I'm meek enough
and bare enough,
open enough
and honest enough
do I begin to understand
I am bountifully blessed with more than enough.

As soon as I inflate myself,
adorn myself,
disguise myself
or shield myself
I'm less than what I am,
and I begin to shrivel.

Pare me down to plain and simple
so I can understand
the magnificence of modesty
and the defenseless power
of nakedness.
Take me to that humble place
where I can fully feel
the promise of abundance.

LET IT SHINE

All of it is mine
from frivolous to oh so fine…
the dark and dreadful,
the wondrous and witty,
the brilliant and bumbling,
the shy and shitty.
When I push a piece of me
underneath or over there,
back behind or anywhere
it always finds a wily way
to slither out and make me pay.

Give me the courage to open wide
and see my shadow side.
Give me guts to view the savage stuff
and still know I'm enough.
Give me strength to hold my mangled mess
and weave it into quite a dress.
Give me poise to take the golden glow
and boldly let it show.
Give me faith to wear what's mine
and let it shine,
to welcome all of me
and set my spirit free.

DOWNWARD MOBILITY

More and more and then some more
is nothing more than more.
More is rarely better.
More is simply more.

When all that is accumulated
fails to fill and fascinate,
look at all the emptiness
buried underneath.

Giving up on keeping up
opens up the way
to letting go and letting love
fill us every day.

Filling in the Gap

We inhabit the gap
between that which is real
and that which we hope is possible.

We live in a war torn world
yet encounter moments of peace.

We endure political strife
yet experience hints of harmony.

We witness cultures clashing
yet sense the notion of oneness.

We see discrimination
yet strive toward justice for all.

Give us tools to fill in the gap
between that which is real
and that which we hope is possible.

Living and Breathing

When you are hanging by a thread
take a breath.
Then think sew what?
When you are limping along
take a breath.
Then step into another place.
When you are missing the big picture
take a breath.
Then draw on everything.
When you are hitting all the wrong notes
take a breath.
Then sing another song.
When you have no easy answers
take a breath.
Then ask a different question.
When you are under the gun
take a breath.
Then shoot for the moon.
When you are tied in knots
take a breath.
Then loosen the laces.
When you are scared to death
take a breath.
Then leap into life!

SEE THROUGH

A should
is thrown on
like a Victorian velvet cape
heavy laden
with responsibility
and bordered
with buttons of ought,
but a could
is created
out of sheer imagination
and gossamer possibilities
transparent enough
to see through.
If we only do
what we should
we might not see
what we could.

DANCE WITH YOURSELF

Dance away from expectations
and spin into the space
where you can be yourself
wallowing in the wonder
of how you found this place.
Who's that person underneath?
Nervous Nellie?
Stable Stan?
Wonder Woman!
Superman!
Stripped of expectations
how do you see yourself?
Draped in worry?
Caped in fear?
Bare and brazen?
Free and clear?
You will be your partner
when you dance around this place.
It might be kind of scary.
It might be kind of fun.
It might be something like
you've never ever done.
Just dance and dance and dance some more
until you find the you in you
waltzing 'round the floor.

A Lesson From My Tree

I see my tree
standing in the circle.
She talks to me
whenever I take the time to listen.
My tree is filled with fearlessness.
The world rustles through her branches,
and her roots rest in infinity.
She has weathered many storms
and lost a bough or two.

My tree doesn't preach.
Her mere existence is an example
of the ancient law of life.
Her strength is trust
for every winter there is death,
and every spring rebirth.
Season after season
she trusts that she is living
the holy life of tree.

Oh, if I could be my tree,
but the sound of falling leaves
drops a message in my ear.

I hear her loud and clear.
I cannot be my tree,
but maybe I can learn from her
to trust that I am living
the holy life of me.

THE UPPER LAKE

(The poem my mother requested for her funeral)

I walk along the wooded path
  that leads to a sacred spot
  flooded with the past,
  drenched in the present,
  and spilling over into the future.
The surface ripples with reflections
  reminding me that what I see
  mixes memory with reality.
The lake lined with evergreens
  is dotted with demise
  of ancient hemlocks older than I.
Death makes me want to cry
  when I see the naked limbs
  stranded in the sky.
 But when I bow my head
  and see the barren branches
  mirrored in the water,
  the blight is blurred
  and death is beautifully blended in.
I don't know what I was looking for
  when I came to the lake today,
  yet I always find something
  floating up and sinking in.

This family piece of peace
　　is one of those thin places
　　that feels like multiple spaces
　　spliced together with mystery
　　and pointing to eternity.

Dark before Dawn

Awakened
by an unknown sound,
she lies alone in the dark
with unsolicited thoughts.

The quiet
grows a little louder
as uninvited questions
whir around inside her.

The nagging worries
buzzing through her brain
swell into a hornet's nest
filled with stinging repercussions.

In the bright of day
her mind is clearer,
but darkness
holds another kind of logic.

If only the slow, steady tick
of the bedside clock
would quicken to this pace
of swooping worriment!

But the morning sun cannot be hurried.
This night will pass as every night before,
no more swiftly for this restless soul,
no more slowly for that peaceful dreamer.

In time the day will break.
Then light will shine,
and soundness will return.

HELP

Help me
hold what I cannot heal
and tolerate the pain.
Help me
hear the desperate cry
and blot away the hopelessness.
Help me
drop my own defenses
and pick up all the broken pieces.
Help me
peer through blind spots
and see the heart of the matter.
Help me
find a chord of comfort
and sing a song of reassurance.
Help me.
Help me.
Help me
help.

SEEING IN THE DARK

I remember rocking along,
feeling I was in control
when all at once
I skidded into darkness
and couldn't find my way.
Not my choice
to be in such a spot
for no one ever chooses
disorder and distress.
In this place of chaos
I was thrown for quite a loop.
I couldn't see ahead
so I had to open up
and trust whatever brought me here
to guide me through the shadows.
While wandering in the dark
I seemed to pick up something
I never would have seen
while blinded by the light.

STAY AND BE STILL

I find myself lost
wandering
roaming through
an unfamiliar space
a very valuable place
filled with findings
undiscovered
and remnants
disremembered.
I must stay and be still
listen
watch
wonder
wait
until I feel the shift
from being lost
to being present.
After awhile
I find a piece
of faint forgotten
glowing
in the distance
drawing me
in a new direction.

LOOKING FOR THE SUNNY SIDE

Keep on the sunny side,
always on the sunny side.
The notes are in the air.
The tune is always there,
but lately I've been pulled
to the other side of life -
the shadow side of death,
the dense side of grief,
the somber side of sick,
the dark side of fear.
Although I'm in a backslide
I know there is a bright side.
The notes are in the air.
The tune is always there
so even in the black of night
I'm looking for the sunny side of life.

My Uninvited Guest

Now I lay me down to sleep
with worry
as my uninvited guest.
I yearn to send the caller packing,
but bother
seems to feel content
to keep my rapt attention.
May as well say welcome,
but midnight hospitality
fails to flow from me.
Be gone, be gone
disquiet and distress!
Take leave of me.
I need my rest.
Slip away
and let me slide
out of fear and fright
into the deep of dream,
out of haunted night
into morning's beam.

MAKING LOVE TO THE MEMORIES

Alone in bed
she strokes the wrinkled sheet
pulling the memories
up from the deep
to hold her for awhile.
A faint voice
still hoarse with morning sleep
utters words of arousal.
She reaches for an unseen hand
remembering the feel of his fingers
coming together with her fingers,
his thumb making its way
around her palm,
her nails stroking his freckled skin.
His absent body
is cradled in her being.
Reaching for the empty space
she makes love to the lingering memories,
powerful,
pulsing,
bittersweet love.

THE OTHER SIDE

If you can tell me
where I'm going
after I leave here,
I won't be
going there.
The other side
of life is
mystery.
It's not an up
or down there.
I'm going somewhere
that cannot be described
in terms of time and space
and who will be there
and who will not.
I'm simply going
to what will be...

THE GARDEN AND THE POOL

Where did she want her ashes scattered?
First the garden in the churchyard,
following the routine ritual.
The priest recited written words
heard every time
remains of strangers,
friends and relatives
are planted in the ground.
We mixed her in the soil of souls
as part of something holy and mysterious
but saved a bit of her
and travelled to the hidden pool
where water falls and mystery lives,
and written prayers are never needed.
We filled our glass with spirits
to toast her love that lives among us.
We blessed the bountiful beauty
then scattered her in the deep.

AN EMPTY PLACE

I walked into her yellow room
and had to catch my breath.
The bed that held her
when she left us
was gone.
The chairs that held us
when we watched her go
were gone.
I stood in the empty place,
eyes full of tears
and heart full of loss.
The vacant room
devoid of her belongings
and brimming with her essence
sent me looking
for something to fill
the awful gaping hole.
I reached for a photo album
filled with pages
pointing to the past,
and the emptiness in me
began to fill with memories.

Beyond Endings

here we are

trapped in calendar time
cooped in earthly space

but deep in the depths
lies a holy invisible place

a realm without endings
where one and all began

an eternal sphere
filled with unfathomable grace

pulling us in
to the everlasting embrace

WORRY WOMAN TRANSFORMED

The slow, methodical ring
is out of step with the thump-thump
beat pulsing in my chest
as I return the medical madam's call.
I hear a hint of disappointment
in her bloody recitation
informing me the genes they tested
were negative and normal.
I'm useless to the scientist
as subject to be studied.
I interrupt her rote recital
with a happy hallelujah!
Both mounds can stay upon my chest,
no brutal slashing necessary,
no painful reconstruction.
The best of all however
is these genes, not gender biased,
will not be passed along
to my sons and to their children,
to my siblings and their offspring,
to the ones I love so dearly.
A weight is lifted from my chest
while nature's weights will still remain.
The news is absolutely powerful
transforming me from Worry Woman

into Wonder Woman,
bald and bold, diseased and yet determined!
A lump removed and radiation
what a piece of cake!
I kiss my loving husband
and place his caring hands
upon my sagging breasts
to lift them up and celebrate,
to smile instead of weep
over what we get to keep!

DISTILLING IT DOWN

Caught in a mountain of wordy woes
I tried to shrink it down
to simple, single syllables.
Preferring concise
I took the advice
of a wise and wonderful woman
who taught me when I pray
all I need to say is
HELP or WOW or THANKS.
HELP came out quite easily,
and WOW was a form of fuck.
I stumbled and bumbled
with THANKS for awhile
not feeling the slightest rumble.
But the power I felt with WOW,
and the more I cried for HELP
a tumble of THANKS rolled over me...
for family and friends,
for medical marvels,
for readers I don't even know,
for Anne Lamott
who gave me these words
as a pointed way to pray.

HELP, WOW, THANKS
is all I need to say,
and when I devoutly
distill it down
I simply bow in
silence.

The Shedding Season

Weariness is my companion
dragging me through
a browner shade of autumn,
lacking all the vibrancy
of last year's gold and crimson.
The faded color of exhaustion
washes over everything,
and there is nothing left to do
but rest and be with me.
I must be gentle with myself
and learn from nature's shedding season,
embrace my temporary baldness
and join the mighty oaks
who bare their solid structure
as they shed their outer cover.
Like trees who drop their autumn leaves
in wait and preparation
I'll drop my hurried pace
and fill it full of dormant space.

THANKSGIVING

Let us carve away complaints
and stuff ourselves with gratitude,
set aside our troubles
and taste abounding joy.

Let us slice through greediness
and find a way to feed the starving,
cut through all our neediness
and satisfy that inner hunger.

Let us scrape away the troubled past
and feast on pleasant memories,
wash away the weariness
and see the gifts the years have given.

Let us put aside our differences
and toast to our togetherness
then sing a song of thanks
for the presence of each other
and the nourishment of life.

Grieving and Grateful

Father, mother, sister's husband,
husband's friend, and little westie
all are scattered here at Sapphire
in water, woods and grassy ground.
Then there are those I do not know
like bear and deer, goose and heron,
rainbow, bass and brim
who roam and fly and swim and die
in what is home to them.
In this place
I feel a sense of animal contentment.
Mother Nature reminds me
nothing remains forever.
Ashes to ashes, dust to dust.
I'm grieving for the gone
yet grateful for all around me,
feel what I have lost
yet know what still surrounds me.
What was here and what is now
is spawning what will be.

A DARK YEAR

That year's canvas
was filled with darker hues
of suffering and loss
shedding more shadow than light.
The color of death
permeated the piece
leaving jagged splashes of grief
softened with strokes of relief.
When a lump of disease
distorted the surface
the picture exuded exhaustion.
That year's painting is done,
but next year's canvas awaits
to be filled with altered colors
in various shades of healing
and brighter blushes of hope.

DIMINISHED AND ENLARGED

She is different now
than she was then.
There is less of her,
but somehow there is more.
The lump
was carved away
leaving a hole
to be filled
with something unseen
yet deeply felt.
What is gone
is nothing more
than deadly flesh.
What is gained
is filled
with living spirit.
Here she is
somewhat diminished
and somehow enlarged.

INHALING HOPE

Before I step into the bath
I gaze at my reflection
and see a winter tree,
twisted, misshapen, exposed,
a haunting skeleton displayed.
As dusk dissolves to black
I cover my bony branches
in tender, wooly warmth
and wait for sleep to shield me through the night.
When dawn gives birth to blue
streaked with pastel whimsy
I see the trees outside my window
in early morning frost coats.
The diamond twigs shiver and creak
until the source of light
melts away the winter garments
worn for sheer protection.
A sudden breath of warmer wind
fired by noon day brilliance
whispers to the naked boughs
a promise billowing with blossom.
The leafless limbs inhale the hope
of emerald resurrection
as sunset colors wash the sky
in vivid confirmation.

A Silver Spring

Outside her windowpane
she sees the colors of spring.
Yellow sprinkled through the woods,
and hints of various greens
are sending nature's promise
of what will come to be.

Reflected in her mirror
she sees her color of spring.
The scalp is sprouting something new
in various shades of grey,
a sparkling silver promise
of blossoming health and hope.

TIME AFTER TIME

Time after time
they washed the dinner dishes,
wiped the kitchen counter
and corked the Cabernet.
The soothing supper music
was mixed with clanging pans
being placed where they belonged.
A night like any other...
or so she thought.
Then he took her in his arms,
and the kitchen clatter faded
as the music drew them in.
She placed her wrinkled cheek
on his soft cotton shoulder
as they swirled between
the sink and stove
and waltzed around the oven.
His hurting seemed to heal
and her disease dissolve.
They were really cookin',
and the aches and pains took wing
as two old married lovers swayed
to Time after Time.

MY SONS

I gave birth to them.
They give life to me.

I fancy their humor,
value their views,
cherish their children,
relish their news.

When I have fallen down,
their steady hands pull me up.
When I have fallen to pieces,
their embraces hold me together.

As little boys
I cared for them
then set them free.
Now on their own,
they care for me.

My Daughters

In law
Grand
Step
In law
Grands
leapt
into my life.
I love every one of them,
but I gave birth to none of them.
Thanks to the men in my life
for giving me my daughters.

TEARS TRANSFORMING

When pain and anguish
rained on me
you held my hand
and took me through
the storm of suffering.
You bathed my eyes
in burning tears
transforming into golden drops
of glittering gratitude.
I never would have asked for such,
but nonetheless I gained so much.
You washed me in amazement
and showered me with wonder,
blew my mind wide open,
and filled my battered body
with unexpected blessings.

CELEBRATION

Let us celebrate this day
For the priceless gift of time
For the joyful sound of laughter
For the taste of something new
For the feel of old and worn
For the noise of mother nature
For the quiet of solitude
For unexpected relief
For unconditional love
For the presence of each other
For the miracle of being

A Colorful Resurrection

'Tis time to wave goodbye
to winter's dormant stillness
and awaken to a colorful resurrection.

As tiny little blossoms
brighten vinca vines
with purple-blue embellishment
may our winter blues be brightened.

As golden yellow daffodils
undulate and sway
in the gusty winds of March
may our minds be swayed by something new.

As clustered patches of pink
adorn the barren branches
of weeping cherry trees
may spring adorn our souls with wonder.

As leaves on dogwoods,
maples, oaks and birches
open up in different shades of green
may our hearts be open to various shades of being.

'Tis time to blossom,
to dance into the colorful newness
and sing a song of spring!

MY INVISIBLE DESTINATION

I cannot know when I will reach
　　my invisible destination.
Whether it be near or far
　　it lies over
　　　　and beyond.

What awaits around the bend
　　while in the here and now?
Will I step into surprise
　　that lifts me up and makes me soar
　　　　or stumble over something
　　　　　　that shakes me to the core?
Will I travel with a carefree step
　　thinking my footprints will disappear
　　　　like tracks in squishy sand?
Or will I stride with confidence
walking hand in hand with truth
feeling my mark might make a dent?

Whether walking assuredly
　　or wandering about,
　　　　I'll count upon my guide
　　　　　　to infuse each step with quiet courage
　　　　　　　as I move a little closer
　　　　　　　　to my invisible destination.

DAZZLE OF DRAGONFLIES

flying on wisdom wings
a dazzle of dragonflies
comes swooping out of nowhere
with a message of transformation
swarming through the air

darting
twisting
turning
a multitude of sizes
some are going backwards
when the need arises

oh you ancient insects
wing your way of wisdom
and reflect the power of light
turn my dark illusions
into bits and dabs of bright

THE BEAUTIFUL STRANGER

I was waiting in line at Mojo Burrito
with nothing on my head
but silver sprouts
barely beginning to curl.
A beautiful dark skinned woman
turned and looked at me
then quickly twirled away.
She turned again and spoke
complimenting my hair.
I thanked her for the kindness
confessing the sprouted style
was not a matter of choice.
Hers was under wraps
tied in a blue bandana
covered with a cap.
She described her hidden locks
as a massive mess of magenta
she wanted to whittle down.
Strangers laughing and talking hair,
she with more than plenty
and I with little or less.
She ordered food to go
then settled up and left.

The cashier then surprised me
saying I didn't owe a cent
for the woman in front of me
had paid my tab in full.
I raced to the door
and called to the beautiful stranger
across the parking lot.
She turned and waved then headed to her car.
I who have more than plenty
salted my quesadilla
with involuntary tears.

The Healing Winds of Iona

Somewhere out of nowhere
I found myself
leaping over the sea waves
splashing onto the ferry ramp.
My trusty shoes with purple laces
had landed in Iona.
I walked between
my husband and my sister
following friends and strangers
to the gate of St. Columba.
Early on I found
I lacked the energy
to cover all the ground
beneath my curious feet,
but my heart was satisfied.
My eyes took in
whatever crossed my path...
little lambs and buttercups,
daffodils and ancient stone.
Every breath of Scottish air
filled my lungs
with longing and with gratitude.
My ears took in the sound of wind
and the sound of song,
the sound of rain and laughter.

My body devoured delicious fare,
and my mind digested food for thought.
I was on a celebration journey
to the center of my sacred world.
Now that I am home
my world is filled with pilgrims
who seeped into my heart
like characters in a novel who enter me
and become an integral part
of who and what I am.
The healing winds of Iona
have blown me in a new direction.
I bow. I bow, and then I bow again.

THE PILGRIMAGE OF LIFE

Every day
we take another step
on the pilgrimage of life
looking for bits and pieces
of who we want to be.
We find a little here.
We find a little there.
Sometimes we forget
what we had found before.
Oftentimes we come across
unsightly snips and scraps
we'd rather not inspect,
but let us bend and pick them up,
carry them around
and hold them for awhile.
Those lovely buried bits
and shameful snarly snips
that make us who we are
can be so hard to find
for part of us is hiding,
and part of us is blind.
But never let us give up searching
for everything we're seeking
is indeed already there.

IMPROVISATION

spontaneous
diverging
without thinking
without knowing
just moving
just going
the impossible
implausible
incredible
all within my range
while caught in the soaring treble
above the grounded refrain
then diving through the bass
and bathing in the blues
an unfamiliar sound emerges
deeper
darker
fuller than before
fluid notes and fertile chords
purring and roaring
delving and soaring
in and around the tune
diving through the earth
and swimming to the moon

GRIEF REKINDLED

We shared so much
throughout the years
including our looks and name.
Knowing her taught me love.
Losing her brought me pain.
The fiery flame of grief
over losing one so dear
always gets rekindled
as the Hallmark day draws near.
There is no Mom to wine and dine.
There is no Mom to call,
but memories I have
of the mother I love
help carry me through it all.

WONDERINGS

I wonder
if my words
have made a difference,
if my heart
has held another's pain,
if my eyes
have glimpsed the glory,
if my ears
have heard the laughter,
if my thoughts
have found a missing piece,
if my feet
have walked in someone else's shoes.
I wonder
if I've grabbed the joy and touched the sorrow.
Have I lived as if there's no tomorrow?